Northern New England

Maine
New Hampshire
Vermont

John Ziff

Mason Crest
450 Parkway Drive, Suite D
Broomall, PA 19008
www.masoncrest.com

©2016 by Mason Crest, an imprint of National Highlights, Inc.

Printed and bound in the United States of America.

CPSIA Compliance Information: Batch #LES2015.
For further information, contact Mason Crest at 1-866-MCP-Book.

First printing
1 3 5 7 9 8 6 4 2

Library of Congress Cataloging-in-Publication Data

Ziff, John.
Northern New England : Maine, New Hampshire, Vermont / John Ziff.
pages cm. — (Let's explore the states)
Includes bibliographical references and index.
ISBN 978-1-4222-3330-6 (hc)
ISBN 978-1-4222-8615-9 (ebook)
1. Northeastern States—Juvenile literature. 2. Maine—Juvenile literature.
3. New Hampshire—Juvenile literature. 4. Vermont Juvenile literature. I. Title.
F106.Z55 2015
974—dc23

2014050185

Let's Explore the States series ISBN: 978-1-4222-3319-1

Publisher's Note: Websites listed in this book were active at the time of publication. The publisher is not responsible for websites that have changed their address or discontinued operation since the date of publication. The publisher reviews and updates the websites each time the book is reprinted.

About the Author: Writer and editor John Ziff lives near Philadelphia.

Picture Credits: Office of the Governor of New Hampshire: 34; Library of Congress: 15, 20, 32, 33, 35 (top), 38 (left), 53, 58 (top; bottom left); Dominic D'Andrea/National Guard Heritage Collection: 17; New Hampshire Historical Society: 38 (top right); used under license from Shutterstock, Inc.: 1, 5 (top), 6, 9, 10 (bottom), 13, 16, 19, 21, 24, 25, 27, 28 (main) 29, 30, 37, 39, 40, 41, 44, 45, 47, 48, 49, 50, 52, 54, 55, 56, 57, 59; American Spirit / Shutterstock.com: 5 (bottom), 10 (top), 18, 36 (top); S. Bukley / Shutterstock.com: 58 (bottom right); Featureflash / Shutterstock.com: 38 (bottom right); Frontpage / Shutterstock.com: 36 (bottom); Erika J Mitchell / Shutterstock.com: 51, 60; United Nations photo: 35 (bottom); U.S. Mint: 28 (inset).

Table of Contents

KEY ICONS TO LOOK FOR:

Words to Understand: These words with their easy-to-understand definitions will increase the reader's understanding of the text, while building vocabulary skills.

Sidebars: This boxed material within the main text allows readers to build knowledge, gain insights, explore possibilities, and broaden their perspectives by weaving together additional information to provide realistic and holistic perspectives.

Research Projects: Readers are pointed toward areas of further inquiry connected to each chapter. Suggestions are provided for projects that encourage deeper research and analysis.

Text-Dependent Questions: These questions send the reader back to the text for more careful attention to the evidence presented there.

Series Glossary of Key Terms: This back-of-the book glossary contains terminology used throughout this series. Words found here increase the reader's ability to read and comprehend higher-level books and articles in this field.

LET'S EXPLORE THE STATES

Atlantic: North Carolina, Virginia, West Virginia

Central Mississippi River Basin: Arkansas, Iowa, Missouri

East South-Central States: Kentucky, Tennessee

Eastern Great Lakes: Indiana, Michigan, Ohio

Gulf States: Alabama, Louisiana, Mississippi

Lower Atlantic: Florida, Georgia, South Carolina

Lower Plains: Kansas, Nebraska

Mid-Atlantic: Delaware, District of Columbia, Maryland

Non-Continental: Alaska, Hawaii

Northern New England: Maine, New Hampshire, Vermont

Northeast: New Jersey, New York, Pennsylvania

Northwest: Idaho, Oregon, Washington

Rocky Mountain: Colorado, Utah, Wyoming

Southern New England: Connecticut, Massachusetts, Rhode Island

Southwest: New Mexico, Oklahoma, Texas

U.S. Territories and Possessions

Upper Plains: Montana, North Dakota, South Dakota

West: Arizona, California, Nevada

Western Great Lakes: Illinois, Minnesota, Wisconsin

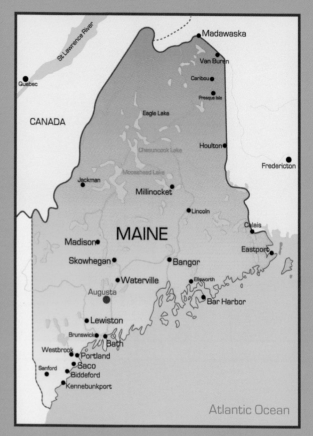

Maine at a Glance

Area: 35,380 sq mi (91,634 sq km).
39th largest state[1]
Land: 30,843 sq mi (79,883 sq km)
Water: 4,537 sq mi (11,751 sq km)
Highest elevation: Mount Katahdin,
5,268 feet (1,606 m)
Lowest elevation: sea level

Statehood: March 15, 1820
(23rd state)
Capital: Augusta

Population: 1,330,089
(41st largest state)[2]

State nickname: the Pine Tree State
State bird: chickadee
State flower: white pine cone

[1] *U.S. Geological Survey*
[2] *U.S. Census Bureau, 2014 estimate*

Maine

In April 2014, the Gallup Organization released the results of a 50-state poll. Gallup asked residents of each state whether they would like to move to another state. Maine residents were the least inclined to relocate.

It's not difficult to understand why. Maine is a beautiful place, with dramatic scenery and an abundance of unspoiled land. Its cities are clean and safe and have a small-town feel. Recent statistics show that Maine has the lowest rate of violent crime in the nation. Maine ranks among the top 10 states for the overall health of its residents. In short, the Pine Tree State has much to offer.

Geography

Maine is located in the far northeastern part of the United States. It borders New Hampshire on the west. The Canadian province of Quebec lies to the northwest. New Brunswick, another Canadian province, is Maine's neighbor to the northeast. On the south and east, Maine is bounded by the Gulf of Maine, a large gulf of the Atlantic Ocean that extends from Cape Cod in Massachusetts to Cape Sable in the Canadian province of Nova

Scotia. Maine's coastline is jagged and, in most places, rocky. Maine has more than 3,100 offshore islands, though the majority cover less than one acre.

At more than 35,000 square miles (91,600 square kilometers) in total area, Maine is roughly the same size as the other five New England states (Connecticut, Massachusetts, New Hampshire, Rhode Island, and Vermont) combined. It ranks as the 39th largest state in the country.

Maine has three major land regions: the Coastal Lowlands, the Eastern New England *Upland*, and the Appalachian Mountains. The Coastal Lowlands region extends

 # Words to Understand in This Chapter

abolitionist—a person who favored the elimination of slavery.

Algonquian—a family of American Indian languages previously spoken in the eastern part of North America.

annex—to take possession of territory and incorporate it into an existing country or state.

envoy—a person empowered to represent a government in specific dealings with another government.

heir—a person who inherits property, usually from a deceased relative.

plateau—an area of relatively flat land that rises sharply above adjacent land on at least one side.

ratify—to approve something (such as a treaty or constitutional amendment) formally.

referendum—a public vote on a particular issue or proposed law.

salt marsh—a coastal wetland that receives salt water from incoming ocean tides.

textiles—fabrics manufactured by weaving or knitting.

tidal creek—a stream that is affected by the ebb and flow of ocean tides.

uplands—elevated land at a significant distance from the sea.

Acadia National Park is one of the first places in the continental United States to see the sunrise.

Atlantic surf crashes on the rocky coast at Portland Head Lighthouse. Completed in 1791, it is the oldest lighthouse in Maine. The lighthouse is still operational, although today it is fully automated.

Boats in Portland Harbor, with the city skyline in the background. Portland is the largest city in Maine, with more than 66,000 residents. The modern city is located at the site of one of the earliest European settlements in Maine, established in 1633.

View of Mount Katahdin, the highest point in Maine. (In the language of the Penobscot Indians, the word Katahdin *means "The Greatest Mountain.") The granite mountain is considered to be the northern end of the Appalachian Trail, a hiking trail that goes all the way to Georgia.*

inland from the Atlantic Ocean. It ranges from about 10 to 40 miles (16 to 64 km) wide, with the widest part occurring in the north. The land is mostly flat and at or near sea level in elevation. In the south, the shoreline features sandy beaches. Rocky beaches, coves, and inlets overlooked by cliffs are found to the north. Inland the Coastal Lowlands contain many *salt marshes* and *tidal creeks*.

West and north of the Coastal Lowlands is the Eastern New England Upland region. This band of territory, ranging from approximately 20 to 50 miles (32 to 81 km) wide, runs northeast through the center of the state. In northern Maine, it curves westward like a breaking wave. Low-lying land in the eastern part of the uplands region gives way to rolling hills and, in places, mountain ridges. Elevations approach 2,000 feet (610 m) in some areas. A broad, flat area called the Aroostook *Plateau* covers the northeastern part of Maine's uplands. The plateau generally has elevations between 800 and 1,000 feet (244 and 305 m). It contains some of Maine's

Did You Know?

Mainers refer to the coastal region from Penobscot Bay to the border with Canada as "Down East." That may seem odd, given that the region represents the northern—or upper—half of Maine's coast. But the term *Down East* originated with sailors. To reach Maine, ships sailing out of Boston traveled downwind and eastward.

most fertile soil and is a center of agriculture. Throughout the uplands, small lakes, rivers, and streams are abundant.

Maine's Appalachian Mountain region covers the western part of the state. Ranges include the White Mountains, which extend into Maine from New Hampshire, and the Blue Mountains. More than a dozen peaks rise above 4,000 feet (1,219 m). The highest, Mount Katahdin, is 5,268 feet (1,606 m) above sea level. It's the centerpiece of Baxter State Park, located in north-central Maine's Piscataquis County.

The Appalachian Mountain region also contains Maine's biggest lakes. Covering about 120 square miles (311 sq km), Moosehead Lake, in Piscataquis County, is the largest. In all, Maine has more than 6,000 lakes and ponds.

Some 32,000 miles (51,500 km) of rivers and streams flow through Maine. The Kennebec is Maine's longest river. It flows 170 miles (274 km), rising at Moosehead Lake and emptying into the Gulf of Maine near the city of Bath. Four tributaries combine in east-central Maine to form the Penobscot River. It runs south for nearly 110 miles (177 km) before emptying into Penobscot Bay. The Androscoggin River enters Maine's Oxford County from New Hampshire, flows east for a while, then turns south. It eventually empties into the Kennebec River near the town of Brunswick.

Maine experiences four distinct seasons. Winters are cold and snowy. Summers tend to be humid and warm, but generally not hot. Spring arrives relatively late, and autumn early. Frosts typically occur as late as May or, in northern Maine, June. And thermometers begin dipping below freezing in late September.

Temperatures tend to be milder in the south and along the coast. For example, on an average day in January, Portland will experience a low of 13° Fahrenheit (–11° Celsius) and a high of 31°F (0°C). In a typical winter, about 72 inches (183 cm) of snow falls on Portland. By contrast, Caribou—located in the northern county of Aroostook—gets about 112 inches (285 cm) of snow in a typical winter. In January, Caribou residents can look forward to a bone-chilling average daily low of 1°F (–17°C), and an average daily high of 20°F (–7°C). In July, Caribou's average daily temperature

Like all the New England states, Maine is subject to nor'easters—powerful storms with winds that blow from the northeast, often bringing high amounts of rain or snow. Here, the Nubble lighthouse weathers a coastal snowstorm.

Autumn colors of a wooded lake in southern Maine. Roughly 80 percent of the state is covered with forests, and logging is an important industry in Maine.

range is 55°F to 76°F (13°C to 24°C). July temperatures in Portland are similarly pleasant, with an average low of 59°F (15°C) and an average high of 79°F (26°C).

History

Native people first migrated to what is today Maine around 9500 BCE. By the 1600s, when Europeans first began colonizing the region, various tribes occupied Maine. They included the Abenaki, Maliseet, Passamaquoddy, and Penobscot. All of them spoke a form of *Algonquian*.

Sailing for the king of France, the Italian navigator Giovanni da Verrazano explored Maine's coast in 1524. But eight decades would pass before the first European efforts to establish a colony in the region. In 1604, a French group under the leadership of a nobleman named Pierre Dugua built a settlement on St. Croix Island, near the mouth of the St. Croix River. Three years later, about 100 Englishmen founded the Popham Colony near the mouth of the Kennebec River. The French and English colonies were both soon abandoned, however.

French colonization in present-day Canada proved much more successful. Meanwhile, English colonists gained a foothold in what is today Massachusetts. Both France and England would lay claim to Maine.

In 1622, two Englishmen—Sir Ferdinando Gorges and Captain John Mason—received a large land grant. It included all territory between the Merrimack River (in present-day southern New Hampshire and northeastern Massachusetts) and the Kennebec River. The two eventually split the land, with Mason taking territory in today's New Hampshire and Gorges keeping the territory in Maine.

Charles I, England's king, reaffirmed Gorges's claim to the Province of Maine with a royal charter issued in 1639. Yet the province attracted relatively few settlers. Gorges died in 1647. Five years later, the growing Massachusetts Bay Colony *annexed* (took over) Maine. In 1677, Massachusetts formally bought the deed to Maine from Gorges's *heirs*.

At the time, colonists in New England—along with Indians who were friendly to them—were fighting five Native American tribes. The colonists called the conflict King Philip's War. Many English settlements in Maine were wiped out or abandoned before the war ended in 1678.

In the decades that followed, England and France—and their colonists in North America—became embroiled in a series of wars that also drew Indians into the fighting. Maine was the site of considerable violence. Finally, the English side won decisively in what came to be known among British colonists as the French and Indian War. In the 1763 treaty that officially ended the war, France gave up its claims to all territory on the North American continent, including Maine.

In 1783, the United States officially gained independence from Great Britain as a result of the Revolutionary War. Soon, some people in Maine began calling for independence from

A New England village prepares to fight approaching Native Americans during King Philip's War (1675–1678). For the next 75 years, the natives would ally with the French to fight against British colonists in Maine.

Massachusetts. A *referendum* on whether Maine should separate from Massachusetts was held in 1792. It

Old Fort Western, located on the Kennebec River in Augusta, is a wooden fort built by colonial militia in 1754. It is the oldest surviving colonial fortification in New England. Today, the fort houses a museum.

failed narrowly. Another referendum, held in 1797, passed by a slim margin. But the vote wasn't binding, and Massachusetts balked at letting Maine go.

The War of 1812, another conflict between the British and the United States, proved to be a turning point in the drive for Maine statehood. During the war, British forces attacked and occupied much of coastal Maine. Maine residents believed that their protection wasn't a priority for Massachusetts. In 1819, Mainers voted overwhelmingly for statehood, and this time the Massachusetts legislature agreed.

The United States Congress approved Maine statehood as part of the Missouri Compromise. Maine (where slavery hadn't existed since 1783, when Massachusetts abolished it) would be admitted to the Union as a free state. Missouri would be admitted as a slave state. This would maintain an equal number of free and slave states. On March 15, 1820, Maine became the 23rd state. Its population was about 300,000—nearly double what it had been in 1800.

In 1860, Maine's population stood at more than 628,000. Mainers were fierce **abolitionists**. During the Civil War (1861–1865) some 70,000 Mainers—more than 11 percent of the state's total population—fought for the Union. Nearly 9,400 lost their lives.

In 1977, three tribes—the Maliseet, Passamaquoddy, and Penobscot—sued the state of Maine. The lawsuit claimed that all previous treaties by which the Indians had ceded land in Maine were invalid because the treaties had never been **ratified** by Congress. The Indians sought $25 billion in damages and the return of about 20,000 square miles (51,800 sq km) of land, which would have displaced one-third of Maine's population. The case was eventually resolved out of court. In 1980, Congress passed, and President Jimmy Carter signed, the Indian Land Claims Settlement Act. The law paid the Indians a sum of $81.5 million.

Government

Maine has a two-chamber legislature. The Maine House of Representatives has 151 regular members. In addition, three seats are reserved for Native

The 20th Maine Infantry Regiment's staunch defense of Little Round Top prevented the Confederate Army from gaining control of the high ground, and helped lead to a Union victory at Gettysburg. That battle is considered a turning point of the Civil War.

In 2014, the copper dome at the Maine State House in Augusta—which had a green patina due to long exposure to the weather—was replaced.

Americans—one each for the Passamaquoddy Tribe, the Penobscot Nation, and the Houlton Band of Maliseet Indians. The Native Americans sit on committees and may cosponsor bills. But they cannot vote on legislation.

Under the state constitution, the number of seats in the Maine Senate may vary. It can be 31, 33, or 35.

Senators as well as representatives are elected to two-year terms. No one may serve more than four consecutive terms. But after two years out of office, a legislator becomes eligible to run again.

Mainers elect their governor to a four-year term. No one may serve more than two consecutive terms as governor. As with legislators, however, there are no lifetime term limits for governors.

Maine's delegation in Congress consists of two members of the House of Representatives, in addition to its two U.S. senators.

In presidential elections, Maine is one of only two states (Nebraska is the other) in which the candidate who wins the statewide popular vote does not automatically receive all the electoral votes. The candidate with the most votes statewide is guaranteed two of Maine's four electoral votes. If the other candidate garners more of the popular vote in either of Maine's congressional districts, he or she gets one electoral vote.

The Economy

If there's one product that people associate with Maine, that product would probably be lobsters. Maine lobsters are renowned for their flavor, and about 90 percent of all lobsters caught in the United States come from Maine's waters. Other important products of Maine's commercial fishing industry include herring, halibut, clams, mussels, and scallops.

Maine is the nation's top producer of wild (or low-bush) blueberries. In 2012, more than 91 million pounds were harvested. Maine also ranks among the top three states in potato production. Other important agricultural products include apples and maple syrup.

More than 80 percent of Maine's land is forested. This includes some 5,500 square miles (14,245 sq km) in the North Woods region, which is made up of western Aroostook County and northern Somerset, Piscataquis, and Penobscot counties. The North Woods is the center of Maine's timber industry. Lumber, various wood products, paper, and paper products are manufactured in Maine.

Shipbuilding was a mainstay of Maine's economy in the 1800s, and it remains an important industry today. Other significant products include *textiles*, processed food, and leather.

The harbor at Monhegan Island, which is located 10 miles (16 km) off the coast of Maine. The island has a small year-round population of about 75 people, most of whom make their living fishing or lobstering. The island has no cars or paved roads. In the summer months, tourists can take a ferry from the mainland communities of Boothbay Harbor, New Harbor, and Port Clyde to visit Monhegan Island.

Some Famous Mainers

Born in Portland and educated at Bowdoin College, poet Henry Wadsworth Longfellow (1807–1882) went on to become one of the best-loved American poets of his era.

Lifelong Maine resident Joshua Lawrence Chamberlain (1828–1914), a professor, college president, and state governor, is best known for his heroism leading the 20th Maine Infantry regiment at the Civil War battle of Gettysburg, for which he received the Medal of Honor.

Writer Sarah Orne Jewett (1849–1909) often set her stories in rural New England, particularly her native Maine. She was from South Berwick.

Poet Edwin Arlington Robinson (1869–1935), a three-time Pulitzer Prize winner, grew up in Gardiner.

Rockland was the birthplace of poet and playwright Edna St. Vincent Millay (1892–1950).

Margaret Chase Smith (1897–1995), the first woman to serve in both the U.S. House of Representatives and the U.S. Senate, hailed from Skowhegan.

A U.S. senator and Senate majority leader, George Mitchell (b. 1933) also served as a U.S. special *envoy* for Northern Ireland. In that post the Waterville native helped broker the 1998 Good Friday Agreement, which ended decades of violence in Northern Ireland.

Books such as *Carrie, The Shining*, and *Misery* have won writer Stephen King (b. 1947) legions of fans. The master of horror, suspense, and fantasy fiction is from Portland, and many of his novels and stories are set in New England.

Freeport's Joan Benoit Samuelson (b. 1957) was one of the country's premier distance runners. In 1984, when the first women's Olympic marathon was held, Samuelson took home the gold medal.

Henry Wadsworth Longfellow

Margaret Chase Smith

Joshua Chamberlain

The People

The 2010 U.S. census counted more than 1.3 million Mainers. Well over half live in coastline counties. In much of the North Woods region, meanwhile, the population density is under one person per square mile.

In 2010, according to the Census Bureau, Maine had a higher proportion of non-Hispanic whites than any other state: 94.4 percent. A majority of Mainers are of French/French Canadian, English, or Irish ancestry.

African Americans make up more than 13 percent of the nation's population, according to the Census Bureau. But just 1.3 percent of Maine residents are black. Similarly, while close to 17 percent of the country's people are Latinos, in Maine the figure is only 1.4 percent. Maine also has a significantly smaller proportion of Asians than the country as a whole (1.1 percent versus 5.1 percent).

Major Cities

With more than 66,000 residents, *Portland* is Maine's largest city. Situated on Casco Bay, in southern Maine's Cumberland County, Portland has a long and fascinating

A Maine fisherman throws a lobster trap (also called a pot) overboard.

history. The town—which eventually acquired the name Falmouth—was destroyed by Indian warriors in 1676 during King Philip's War, by a French and Indian force in 1690 during King William's War, and by the British Royal Navy in 1775 during the Revolutionary War. Each time it was rebuilt. Renamed Portland, the town was incorporated in 1786. It served as Maine's state capital in the 1820s.

An important shipping center, Portland was raided by Southern naval forces during the Civil War. In 1866, Independence Day celebrations touched off a devastating fire that consumed about 1,800 buildings and left more than 10,000 residents homeless. Yet again, the city was rebuilt.

Today's Portland consistently appears on lists of the best places in the country to live. It's also a magnet for visitors who are attracted by its beautiful setting, historic landmarks, thriving arts scene, and multitude of trendy restaurants.

Lewiston is located on the eastern bank of the Androscoggin River in Androscoggin County. With a population of more than 36,000, it's Maine's second largest city.

The county seat of Penobscot County, *Bangor* (2010 population: 33,039) sits on the Penobscot River some 30 miles (48 km) north of Penobscot Bay. It's a transportation hub for southern Maine.

Augusta, located on the Kennebec River in Kennebec County, has been Maine's capital city since 1827. The 2010 census counted 19,136 residents.

Further Reading

Gratwick, Harry. *Hidden History of Maine.* Charleston, SC: The History Press, 2010.

Griffin, Nancy. *Maine 101: Everything You Always Wanted to Know About Maine and Were Going to Ask Anyway.* 2nd ed. Lunenburg, Nova Scotia, Canada: MacIntyrePurcell Publishing, 2013.

Heinrichs, Ann. *Maine.* Rev. ed. New York: Children's Press, 2014.

Internet Resources

http://maineanencyclopedia.com/

Maine: An Encyclopedia includes a wide array of entries about the Pine Tree State.

http://www.maine.gov/sos/kids/about/index.htm

The Department of the Secretary of State of Maine maintains fun and informative online resources for kids.

http://www.mainememory.net/mho/

Maine History Online, a project of the Maine Historical Society, includes a detailed timeline.

http://www.netstate.com/states/geography/me_geography.htm

This site provides detailed information about Maine's geography.

Text-Dependent Questions

1. What is Algonquian?
2. What was the Missouri Compromise, and how did Maine statehood figure in it?
3. Name Maine's largest city.

Research Project

Maine and Nebraska are the only states that don't automatically award all their electoral votes to the presidential candidate who receives the largest share of the popular vote. Find out what electoral votes are. What formula is used to determine the number of electoral votes each state is assigned? How many electoral votes are needed to win the presidency? How many times has a candidate lost the nationwide popular vote but still become president? Present your findings in a short report. Where possible, include charts, graphs, or other visual aids.

New Hampshire at a Glance

Area: 9,349 sq miles (24,214 sq km).
46th largest state[1]
  Land: 8,953 sq mi (23,188 sq km)
  Water: 396 sq mi (1,026 sq km)
Highest elevation: Mount
  Washington, 6,288 feet (1,917 m)
Lowest elevation: Atlantic Ocean,
  sea level

Statehood: June 21, 1788 (9th state)
Capital: Concord

Population: 1,326,813
  (42nd largest state)[2]

State nickname: the Granite State
State bird: purple finch
State flower: purple lilac

[1] *U.S. Census Bureau*
[2] *U.S. Census Bureau, 2014 estimate*

New Hampshire

L ive Free or Die. That's the official *motto* of New Hampshire, a state whose residents pride themselves on their independence and self-reliance.

Geography

New Hampshire is located in the northeastern United States. It borders Quebec on the north, Maine on the east, Massachusetts on the south, and Vermont on the west.

New Hampshire is a small state. It covers less than 9,400 square miles (24,200 sq km). Only four states are smaller.

New Hampshire extends about 190 miles (306 km) from north to south. It's roughly triangular in shape, with the base of the triangle in the south. At its widest point there, the state is about 85 miles (137 km) across. It tapers to about 15 miles

(24 km) across in the north.

Like Maine, New Hampshire consists of three main land regions: the Coastal Lowlands, Eastern New England Upland, and White Mountains. The smallest of these three regions, the Coastal Lowlands, covers the southeastern corner of the state. The region features sandy beaches along New Hampshire's 13-mile (21-km) Atlantic Ocean coast. Inland to a distance of up to 20 miles (32 km) are an assortment of wetlands. The most significant feature is Great Bay. It's a nine-square-mile (23-sq-km) *estuary* fed freshwater by several rivers. Tidal currents from the Atlantic reach Great Bay via the short Piscataqua River (not to be confused with the Maine river of the same name).

West of the Coastal Lowlands is the Eastern New England Upland region. It covers the remainder of southern New Hampshire and extends north through the center of the state. The region contains hills and low mountains, with elevations topping 3,000 feet (914 m) in places. The uplands are also home to many lakes, including the state's largest, Lake Winnipesaukee. It has a surface area

Words to Understand in This Chapter

Continental army—the army of the American colonies that rebelled against British rule during the Revolutionary War.

estuary—a water passage where a river current and ocean tides meet.

high-tech—involving advanced technology, especially electronics and computers.

militia—a group of civilians who train for military service in the event of an emergency.

motto—a short expression that represents a guiding principle.

primary election—an election in which voters determine the candidate from their political party who will run against a candidate from the opposing party for a particular office.

Lake Winnipesaukee in central New Hampshire is a popular vacation spot for tourists.

The White Mountains of New Hampshire in the fall.

The New Hampshire state quarter features a venerable landmark: the Old Man of the Mountain. Discovered in 1805, the granite outcroppings on Cannon Mountain, near the town of Franconia, resembled the profile of a wrinkled old man when viewed from the north. But in May 2003, three years after the minting of the New Hampshire state quarter, the Old Man's familiar visage was lost when part of the formation collapsed.

of about 70 square miles (181 sq km). Other significant features of New Hampshire's Eastern New England Upland region include the Merrimack River valley, which runs in a north-south direction through the middle of the state, and the Connecticut River valley, which is along the border with Vermont.

The rugged White Mountains dominate northern New Hampshire. Their highest peaks are found in the Presidential Range, which is located mostly in Coos County. Mount Washington, at 6,288 feet (1,917 m), is the highest point in New Hampshire. The state's next highest peaks, Mount Adams and Mount Jefferson, both rise above 5,700 feet (1,737 m). The White Mountain region also contains steep valleys.

The Connecticut is New Hampshire's longest river. It runs the length of New Hampshire's border with Vermont. The Merrimack River is formed by the joining of the Pemigewasset and Winnipesaukee rivers at the city of Franklin, in Merrimack County. From there it flows south into Massachusetts. Another major river, the Androscoggin, begins near the town of Errol, where the outflow from Umbagog Lake is joined by the Magalloway River. The Androscoggin flows in a mostly southerly direction before turning east near the town of Gorham and crossing into Maine.

The weather in New Hampshire is famously unpredictable. Sudden storms are common. Daily temperatures often fluctuate wildly. In general, though, the state's climate features long, cold, snowy winters; pleasant spring and fall seasons; and short summers characterized by warm days and cool nights. Statewide, the average

Tugboats guide a cargo ship into Portsmouth Harbor. About five million tons of cargo enter or exit the harbor each year.

Drawbridge over the Piscataqua River, between Portsmouth and Kittery, Maine.

Hikers descend Mount Lincoln, following stone markers that indicate it is part of the Appalachian Trail. The mountain is 5,089 feet (1,551 m) high.

daily low temperature in January is 7°F (–14°C), and the average daily high is 29°F (–2°C). In July, the statewide average daily temperature range is 56°F to 82°F (13°C to 28°C). New Hampshire receives ample precipitation, much of it in the form of snow. Residents of southern New Hampshire can expect four and a half to five feet (137 to 152 cm) of snow in a typical year. Areas in the north may receive twice that amount, or considerably more. On average, about 23 feet (7 m) of snow falls on Mount Washington per year.

History

In 1623, Captain John Mason financed the establishment of the first European colony in what is today New Hampshire. The previous year, the king of England had granted Mason and his friend Sir Ferdinando Gorges the huge parcel of land between the Merrimack and Kennebec rivers. The expedition sent by Mason built two settlements. One was near the mouth of the Piscataqua, at the site of today's town of Rye. The other was about

Did You Know?

On April 12, 1934, winds of 231 miles per hour were recorded at the summit of Mount Washington. For more than 30 years, that stood as the highest wind speed ever measured on earth.

eight miles (13 km) upriver, at Dover. The colony flourished.

Other settlements were soon established. Portsmouth (initially called Strawbery Banke) was founded in 1630. Exeter came into being eight years later. In addition to fishing, settlers generated income by trading with local Indians for furs. At the time, the land that makes up present-day New Hampshire was occupied by various Abenaki bands, including the Cowasuck, Ossipee, Penacook, Pigwacket, Sokoki, and Winnipesaukee.

In 1639, the little settlements dotting the area—which had previously been independent of one another—agreed to unite. But Massachusetts laid claim to the region to its north. By

This drawing from 1705 shows Fort William and Mary, which was built on an island at the mouth of the Piscataqua River to defend New Hampshire and other British colonies in New England. In December 1774, Patriots raided the fort and captured gunpowder, muskets, and cannons that would be used against the British during the American Revolution.

1641, it prevailed in gaining governing authority over the New Hampshire settlements.

New Hampshire became a royal province in 1679, when King Charles II decided to separate it from Massachusetts. But his successor, King James II, folded New Hampshire back into Massachusetts in 1686. James's successors, William and Mary, reversed course once more. In 1691, they decided to make New Hampshire a royal province again. Until 1741, however, the governor of Massachusetts also was governor of New Hampshire.

From the late 1680s until the end of the French and Indian War in 1763, New Hampshire settlers faced repeated raids by hostile Indians and French colonists, and they responded in kind. No major battles were fought on New Hampshire soil, however.

Nor were any battles fought in New Hampshire during the American Revolution (1775–1783). But pro-independence sentiment ran high in New Hampshire. And on January 5, 1776—six months before the signing of the Declaration of Independence—New Hampshire became the first colony to establish a state government independent of Great Britain. During the Revolution, many New Hampshirites fought the British as part of the ***Continental army*** or local ***militias***.

The United States Constitution, which established the U.S. government we know today, was drafted in September 1787. To go into effect, the Constitution required nine states to ratify it. On June 21, 1788, New Hampshire became the ninth state to do so.

John Sullivan, born in Somersworth, was a hero of the American Revolution. He led the raid on Fort William and Mary in 1774, as well as a 1779 expedition against Native Americans allied with the British. Sullivan later served as New Hampshire's governor.

During the 19th century, a thriving textile industry developed in New Hampshire. Most of the mills were situated along the Merrimack River.

Some 34,000 New Hampshire residents fought in the Union army dur-

A 12-year-old girl stands next to a spinning machine in the Amoskeag Manufacturing Company's textile mill in Manchester.

In 2012, Maggie Hassan became the second woman elected governor of New Hampshire. She was elected to a second term in 2014.

ing the Civil War (1861–1865). Meanwhile, the Portsmouth Naval Shipyard built warships for the Union navy.

In the last decades of the 19th century, many New Hampshirites abandoned their farms and migrated west. New Hampshire's unpredictable weather, short growing seasons, and somewhat marginal soil left its farmers hard pressed to compete with farmers in the Midwest.

By the 1920s, New Hampshire's textile industry was also in decline. Mills closed as production moved to the South. New Hampshire's economic fortunes only began to turn around again in the 1960s with the arrival of new businesses, especially in the *high-*

tech industry. After a century of slow growth, New Hampshire's population nearly doubled between 1960 and 1990.

Government

New Hampshire's legislature is called the General Court of New Hampshire. It consists of the 400-seat House of Representatives and the 24-seat Senate. Members of both chambers are elected to two-year terms. There are no term limits.

A couple aspects of New Hampshire's governorship are unusual. First, the governor is elected every two years, instead of every four. Second, the governor's powers are limited by the five-person Executive Council. Its members, too, are elected to two-year terms. The Executive Council may reject the governor's choices to fill administrative positions and judgeships. Its approval is also required on spending matters, including state contracts. No term limits apply to members of the Executive Council or to the governor.

The New Hampshire delegation in

New Hampshire is the only U.S. state that has hosted the formal conclusion of a foreign war. In 1905, delegates from Russia and Japan came to Portsmouth to negotiate and sign a treaty ending the Russo-Japanese War. This photo shows the delegates in session.

In July 1944, representatives of 44 nations met at a resort in Bretton Woods to discuss the establishment of an international financial system. At the Monetary and Financial Conference, the World Bank and International Monetary Fund were established, and the American dollar was designated the standard currency for international exchange.

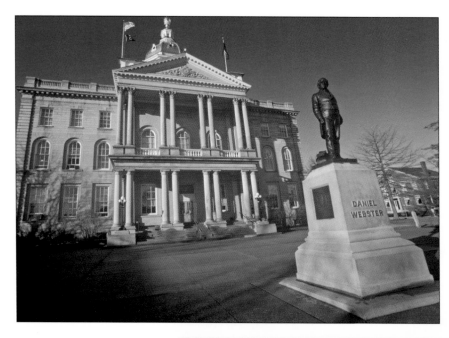

A statue of Daniel Webster stands outside the New Hampshire State House in Concord. Webster was one of the most influential men in the U.S. Congress during the first half of the 19th century.

Hillary Clinton campaigns in Manchester for the Democratic Party's presidential nomination. Because New Hampshire holds the first primary election of the presidential campaign season, candidates spend a large amount of time and money in the small state to make themselves known. A good showing in New Hampshire can boost a candidate's chances of winning his or her party's nomination.

the U.S. Congress consists of two members of the House of Representatives and two senators.

Though it's a small state, New Hampshire plays a big role in presidential politics. That's because New Hampshire is the first state to hold a presidential ***primary election***. Candidates hope to gain momentum by doing well in New Hampshire's primary.

The Economy

New Hampshire is a prosperous state. It consistently ranks among the top 10 states in income per person. And, according to the U.S. Census Bureau, it had the lowest poverty rate in the nation in 2011.

Manufacturing is the main driver of New Hampshire's economy. Overall, more than 9 percent of New Hampshire's workforce was employed in manufacturing as of April 2014. The use of high-tech equipment to make electronic components is particularly important. A recent study found that this specialized sector accounted for nearly one-fifth of all wages paid in the state.

Lighthouse at the entrance to Portsmouth Harbor.

Tourism is another mainstay of New Hampshire's economy. In 2012, visitors spent almost $4.5 billion directly in the Granite State. That year, some 62,000 New Hampshire residents were employed in jobs

Famous People from New Hampshire

Derryfield resident John Stark (1728–1822), who won acclaim as a Revolutionary War general, also provided the words for New Hampshire's state motto: Live Free or Die.

Born and raised in Salisbury (present-day Franklin), Daniel Webster (1782–1852) went on to become one of the most influential statesmen of his era. He represented New Hampshire in the U.S. House of Representatives and Massachusetts in the U.S. Senate, and he served as the nation's secretary of state.

John Stark

The nursery rhyme "Mary Had a Little Lamb" was composed by Newport-born writer and editor Sarah Josepha Hale (1788–1879).

Franklin Pierce (1804–1869), the only U.S. president from New Hampshire, was born and raised in Hillsborough.

Franklin Pierce

Religious leader Mary Baker Eddy (1821–1910) founded the Christian Science movement. She was born in Bow and spent most of her life in New Hampshire.

Sculptor Daniel Chester French (1850–1931), a native of Exeter, is best known for his huge marble statue of Abraham Lincoln at the Lincoln Memorial in Washington, D.C.

In 1961, astronaut Alan Shepard (1923–1998) became the first American to travel into space. Shepard hailed from Derry. Twenty-five years later, in January 1986 Concord schoolteacher Christa McAuliffe (1948–1986) won the opportunity to fly on the space shuttle *Challenger*. McAuliffe and the other six members of the crew perished when the shuttle exploded less than two minutes after liftoff.

The pride of Charlestown, catcher Carlton Fisk (b. 1947) is a member of Baseball's Hall of Fame.

Comedian and actor Sarah Silverman (b. 1970) was raised in Manchester.

Sarah Silverman

View of dormitories at rural Dartmouth College in the Upper Valley of New Hampshire. Founded in 1769, Dartmouth is considered one of the best universities in the United States.

Manchester is a commercial center and the largest city in New Hampshire.

This covered bridge near the village of Bath was built in 1832 over the Ammonoosuc River.

directly or indirectly related to the tourism industry.

New Hampshire's agricultural sector is small, accounting for less than 0.5 percent of the state's total economic output. Apples, dairy products, greenhouse and nursery plants, and Christmas trees are among the leading agricultural products.

The People

The 2010 U.S. census counted a little more the 1.3 million New Hampshire residents. That made New Hampshire the 42nd largest state by population.

New Hampshire is much less racially and ethnically diverse than the country overall. Nationwide, according to the most recent statistics from the Census Bureau, 63 percent of residents are non-Hispanic whites. But in New Hampshire that figure is almost 92 percent. More than 6 in 10 New Hampshirites are of French/French Canadian, English, or Irish ancestry.

African Americans, according to

The Shaker Village at Canterbury is a museum that preserves two dozen buildings from an early New Hampshire community. Shakers were members of a religious sect that established settlements throughout New England during the 18th and 19th centuries.

the Census Bureau, make up less than 1.5 percent of New Hampshire's population. Only 3 percent of the Granite State's residents are Latinos.

Major Cities

With a population of about 110,000, *Manchester* is New Hampshire's largest city. It's located in the southern county of Hillsborough. The Merrimack River, which runs through the city, once powered the textile mills and factories that made Manchester a leading industrial center during the 1800s. Today, Manchester still has about a dozen firms that manufacture various products. It's also a regional center for insurance and finance.

About 87,000 people call *Nashua* home. It, too, is in Hillsborough County, about 15 miles (24 km) south of Manchester. Situated where the Merrimack and Nashua rivers meet, Nashua was once a large mill town. Now it hosts high-tech businesses.

Concord, located on the Merrimack River about 18 miles (29 km) north of Manchester, is New Hampshire's state capital. It's also the county seat of Merrimack County. Concord has a population of more than 42,000.

Further Reading

Auden, Scott. *Voices from Colonial America: New Hampshire 1603–1776*. Des Moines, IA: National Geographic Children's Books, 2007.

Crannell, Karl. *John Stark: Live Free or Die*. Stockton, NJ: OTTN Publishing, 2007.

Heald, Bruce D. *A History of the New Hampshire Abenaki*. Charleston, SC: The History Press, 2014.

Shannon, Terry Miller. *New Hampshire*. New York: Scholastic, 2009.

Internet Resources

http://www.nh.gov/nhinfo

This site, maintained by the New Hampshire State Library, has links to pages on such topics as the state's flora and fauna, government, history, and symbols.

http://www.nhhistory.org/edu/support/nhlearnmore/nhchronology.pdf

The New Hampshire Historical Society is responsible for this historical overview.

http://www.nhstateparks.org

A guide to the Granite State's parks.

http://www.history.com/topics/us-states/new-hampshire

From the History.com website, this page provides facts about New Hampshire, as well as historic photographs of the state.

http://www.netstate.com/states/geography/nh_geography.htm

This site provides detailed information about New Hampshire's geography.

 Text-Dependent Questions

1. Identify New Hampshire's three highest mountains. Do you notice anything about their names?
2. What was especially significant about New Hampshire's decision to ratify the United States Constitution?
3. What special role does New Hampshire play in presidential races?

Research Project

John Stark, whose words became New Hampshire's state motto, had a long and eventful life. Read about Stark. Then write a one-page report focusing on what you find most interesting about him.

Vermont at a Glance

Area: 9,616 sq miles (24,905 sq km). 45th largest state[1]
 Land: 9,216 sq mi (23,869 sq km)
 Water: 400 sq mi (1,036 sq km)
Highest elevation: Mount Mansfield, 4,393 feet (1,339 m)
Lowest elevation: Lake Champlain, 95 feet (29 m)

Statehood: March 4, 1791 (14th state)
Capital: Montpelier

Population: 626,562 (second smallest state)[2]

State nickname: the Green Mountain State
State bird: hermit thrush
State flower: red clover

[1] *U.S. Geological Survey*
[2] *U.S. Census Bureau, 2014 estimate*

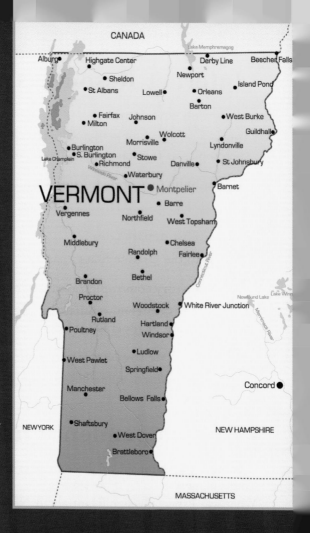

Vermont

The expansion of the United States began with Vermont. After the original 13 states had secured independence by defeating the British in the Revolutionary War, and after they'd established a *republic* through the Constitution, Vermont became the first new state to join the Union.

Geography

At around 9,600 square miles (24,900 sq km) in total area, Vermont is slightly larger than New Hampshire, its neighbor to the east. Vermont also borders Massachusetts to the south, and New York to the west. The Canadian province of Quebec forms Vermont's northern border.

Vermont extends about 160 miles (258 km) from south to north. Unlike New Hampshire, it's narrower in the south and wider in the north. Near the border with Massachusetts, Vermont measures only about 37 miles (60 km) from east to west. It's nearly 90 miles (145 km) across at the border with Quebec.

Vermont's most prominent geographical feature is the source of the state's nickname: the Green Mountain State. Part of the Appalachian chain, the Green Mountains cut through the center of Vermont, dividing the state into eastern and western sections. Five peaks in the Green Mountains rise over 4,000 feet (1,219 m). Among them is Mount Mansfield, the highest point in Vermont at 4,393 feet (1,339 m). It's located in the northern part of the state, along the border of Chittenden and Lamoille counties.

East of the Green Mountains is a geographic region called the Vermont Piedmont. It consists mainly of rolling hills and valleys. The Vermont Piedmont contains many rivers, streams, and lakes, especially in the north. Elevations range from about 300 feet (91 m), in the Connecticut River valley, to 3,114 feet (949 m) at the top of Mount Ascutney. Located in Windsor County, not far from the border with New Hampshire, Mount Ascutney is a *monadnock*—an isolated mountain that rises abruptly from the surrounding land. Overall, elevations in the Vermont Piedmont rise gradually from east to west.

The northeastern corner of Vermont is a rugged region where few people live. Called the Northeastern Highlands, it's considered an extension of New Hampshire's White

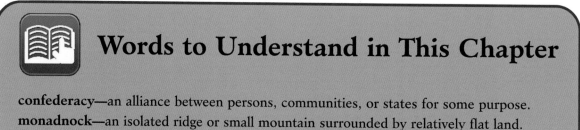

Words to Understand in This Chapter

confederacy—an alliance between persons, communities, or states for some purpose.

monadnock—an isolated ridge or small mountain surrounded by relatively flat land.

republic—a form of government in which citizens elect representatives and a chief executive to exercise governing authority on their behalf; a nation or state with that kind of government.

A creek runs through the Green Mountains of Vermont.

Vermont's Champlain Valley is a region of fertile farmland. The Adirondack mountain range can be seen in the distance.

Aerial view showing colorful fall foliage in the country village of Stowe. Vermont is considered the least urban U.S. state. More than 82 percent of its population lives in rural areas (areas outside of cities or towns) or in small cities with between 2,500 and 50,000 people.

The Champlain Bridge, which opened in 2011, crosses the lake to connect New York and Vermont.

Vermont resorts like Killington, Okemo Mountain, and Smugglers' Notch have long been popular among skiers and snowboarders.

Lake Memphremagog, on the Vermont-Canada border, is a large freshwater lake that covers 41 square miles (110 sq km). The small city of Newport is located on the Vermont shore.

Mountains. Vermont's Northeastern Highlands covers about 600 square miles (1,550 sq km), including most of Essex County and small parts of Caledonia and Orleans counties. The region's most imposing features are scattered granite mountains. Among them are 3,330-foot (1,015-m) Gore Mountain and 3,267-foot (996-m) Burke Mountain, another monadnock.

A lowland region covers northwestern Vermont. Called the Champlain Valley, or sometimes the Vermont Lowlands, it extends eastward from the New York border to the western slopes of the Green Mountains. From north to south, it runs more than half the length of the state, from the Canadian border to the Poultney River. The Champlain Valley contains relatively flat and gently rolling land. Elevations range from under 100 feet (31 m) along Lake Champlain to about 1,800 feet (549 m) in the foothills of the Green Mountains. The Champlain Valley has fertile soil and is

Vermont's most productive farming area.

South of the Champlain Valley, a narrow section of southwestern Vermont is covered by the Taconic Mountains. They extend into Vermont from New York. The region has low hills and cliffs, along with some higher peaks. The highest, Mount Equinox, rises more than 3,800 feet (1,160 m).

Between the Taconic Mountains and the Green Mountains is the Vermont Valley. It is 85 miles (137 km) long and ranges from about one to five miles (1.6 to 8 km) in width. Several rivers cut through the valley.

In addition to the Connecticut River, which forms Vermont's border with New Hampshire, the Green Mountain State's major rivers include Otter Creek, the West River, the White River, and the Winooski River. Otter Creek flows more than 110 miles (177 km) northward through the counties of Bennington, Rutland, and Addison before emptying into Lake Champlain. The 95-mile-long (153-km-long) Winooski begins in northeastern Washington County, flowing southwest past the state capital of Montpelier before turning northwest. It cuts through the Green Mountains

Voters at the Calais Town Hall raise yellow cards to register their vote on Town Meeting Day. In Vermont, each community's local government officers are elected in a town meeting held on the first Tuesday in March.

before emptying into Lake Champlain. The 54-mile (87-km) West River and 60-mile (97-km) White River are both tributaries of the Connecticut River.

Major lakes in the Green Mountain State include Lake Champlain, which Vermont shares with New York and Canada, and Lake Memphremagog, which Vermont shares with Canada. The largest natural lake completely within Vermont is Lake Bomoseen. Located in Rutland County, in the western part of the state, it has a surface area of only about four square miles (10 sq km).

Overall, Vermont's climate is characterized by cold winters with lots of snow, crisp spring and fall seasons, and mild summers. Conditions vary across the state, however. For example, average temperatures are a couple degrees higher in Burlington, located on Lake Champlain, than they are in Montpelier, located in the north-central part of Vermont. Burlington also receives considerably less snow per year than Montpelier—about 81 inches (206 cm) versus 95 inches (241 cm). In January, Montpelier's average daily low is 7°F (–14°C), and its average daily high is 26°F (–3°C). In July, the average daily temperature range is 56°F to 78°F (13°C to 26°C) .

History

In 1609, the French explorer Samuel de Champlain led an expedition south from the recently founded Quebec City. He eventually reached a long lake, which he named for himself. Champlain claimed the area for the French North American colony of New France.

Some of the Native American tribes that inhabited the Vermont region before the arrival of Europeans spent their winters in birch long-houses like this one.

At the time, native peoples were engaged in a long-running conflict for control of the region. The French sided with Abenaki peoples against a powerful *confederacy* of tribes known as the Iroquois (or Haudenosaunee).

In 1666—nearly six decades after Champlain had claimed the region—the French established the first European settlement in present-day Vermont. It was on Isle La Motte, an island in the northern part of Lake Champlain.

In 1723, the Massachusetts colonial legislature ordered the construction of a fort on the Connecticut River in what is today southeastern Vermont. Fort Dummer, which would become Brattleboro, was supposed to help defend Massachusetts from attacks by Abenaki Indians. But a 1741 royal decree fixed the northern border of Massachusetts a few miles south of Brattleboro.

However, the question of which colony owned the land that makes up present-day Vermont remained unclear. New York claimed that its eastern boundary extended all the way

Samuel de Champlain and French soldiers arrive at a river in New France, while Native American porters carry their canoes.

to the Connecticut River. New Hampshire's royal governor reasoned that his colony's western border should align with the western limit of Massachusetts. This would mean New Hampshire's territory extended well past the Green Mountains.

Fort Ticonderoga was a French fort that was captured by the British during the French and Indian War. In May 1775, the Green Mountain Boys commanded by Ethan Allen and Benedict Arnold captured the fort in a surprise attack. Cannons from Fort Ticonderoga were sent to Boston, where George Washington used them to besiege the British troops there. Today, the fort is preserved as a museum and center for historical research.

In 1749, the New Hampshire governor, Benning Wentworth, began issuing land grants in the disputed region. Settlers bought land to establish farms. Eventually, the "New Hampshire Grants," as they were called, amounted to more than 125 townships.

But New York refused to recognize the New Hampshire Grants. And after the end of the French and Indian War in 1763, Britain's king ruled in favor of New York. Land titles in the New Hampshire Grants were voided.

Not everyone accepted the decision, however. By 1770, people who'd bought land in the New Hampshire Grants formed a militia known as the Green Mountain Boys. Under the leadership of Ethan Allen and Seth Warner, the Green Mountain Boys kept New York authorities at bay. They drove settlers from New York out of the remote territory.

When the Revolutionary War broke out, Allen and members of the Green Mountain Boys quickly joined the fight against the British. In May 1775, they helped capture Fort Ticonderoga. The strategic fort was located at the southern end of Lake Champlain. The Green Mountain Boys later formed the core of a Continental army regiment.

In January 1777, representatives from the New Hampshire Grants met in the town of Westminster. They declared their independence—not just from Britain but also from New York. That July, delegates meeting in the town of Windsor approved a constitution. It established the independent Vermont Republic.

Many Vermonters favored joining the United States. But Congress, yielding to pressure from New York, refused to recognize Vermont as independent of New York. Finally, in 1790, New York dropped its objections to Vermont statehood. New York withdrew its territorial claims, and in return Vermont paid New York compensation of $30,000. On March 4, 1791, Vermont became the 14th state admitted into the Union.

Vermont's population expanded dramatically after statehood. In 1790,

This monument commemorates a Revolutionary War battle near Bennington, Vermont, in which the Green Mountain Boys worked with a New England militia commanded by John Stark to defeat a British force in August 1777. The granite obelisk is 306 feet (93 m) tall.

About 80 percent of the farmland in Vermont is used for dairy farming, and about $1.2 billion worth of Vermont milk, cheese, and other dairy products are sold each year.

helped fuel Vermont's growth. Meanwhile, the state's forests were cleared wholesale for new farms and for timber. The result was erosion and a loss of soil fertility.

In the late 1800s, many Vermont farmers abandoned their land and moved west. Population growth slowed. Those trends continued in the first decades of 20th century.

By the mid-1900s, however, Vermont had turned toward more sustainable agriculture and land management practices. An emphasis on environmental protection went hand in hand with a growing tourism industry. A century ago, trees covered just one-quarter of Vermont. Today, forests have been restored to three-quarters of the Green Mountain State.

Government

about 85,000 people lived in Vermont. Ten years later, that number had nearly doubled, to almost 155,000. By 1850, the population had doubled again, to about 314,000.

Industries such as mining, lumber milling, and textile manufacturing

The Vermont General Assembly is a bicameral legislature. The lower house, the Vermont House of Representatives, has 150 members. The upper house, the Vermont Senate, has 30 members. Representatives and senators are each elected to two-year

The Rock of Ages quarry at Barre produces granite used in gravestones throughout the United States. The enormous quarry was opened in 1885; it covers 20 acres and employs more than 200 people. Visitors can tour the facility and find out more about how granite is quarried and used.

terms, with no limits on the number of terms an individual may serve.

Along with neighboring New Hampshire, Vermont is the only state whose governor is elected every two years. No term limits apply.

In the U.S. Congress, Vermont is allotted one seat in the House of Representatives, in addition to its two seats in the Senate.

The Economy

Vermont is famous for its small, independent farms. Yet manufacturing accounts for a considerably larger share of Vermont's economy than agriculture.

Some Famous Vermonters

Ethan Allen (1738–1789) was leader of the Green Mountain Boys militia, an advocate for Vermont independence, and a Revolutionary War hero.

Another hero of the Revolution was Seth Warner (1743–1784), a leader of the Green Mountain Boys who became a colonel in the Continental army.

Born in Rutland, blacksmith John Deere (1804–1886) invented an improved plow and founded the agricultural equipment company that still bears his name.

Joseph Smith (1805–1844), founder of the Church of Jesus Christ of Latter-day Saints, commonly called the Mormon Church, spent his early years in the Vermont town of Sharon.

Admiral George Dewey (1837–1917), a Montpelier native, won fame for his decisive victory at the 1898 Battle of Manila Bay, during the Spanish-American War.

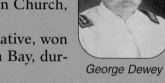

George Dewey

One of America's greatest poets, Robert Frost (1874–1963) taught for 42 years at Middlebury College near Ripton. The small farm where he lived near Ripton, now owned by the college, is open to the public. Frost won the Pulitzer Prize for Poetry four times, and in 1961 was named the first Poet Laureate of Vermont.

Professor and activist Jody Williams (b. 1950), a native of Brattleboro, won the 1997 Nobel Peace Prize for her efforts to have landmines banned.

Waitsfield's Grace Potter (b. 1983) is a singer and multi-instrumentalist. She fronts the band Grace Potter and the Nocturnals.

Pro golfer Keegan Bradley (b. 1986), one of the bright young stars of the PGA Tour, grew up in Woodstock.

Snowboarder Hannah Teter (b. 1987), from Belmont, won an Olympic gold medal at the 2006 Winter Games, and an Olympic silver medal in 2010.

Robert Frost

Hannah Teter

It also employs more people. Among Vermont's leading manufactured products are electronics components; industrial equipment; and paper, furniture, and other wood products.

Vermont's quarries yield high-quality granite, slate, and marble. Talc is also mined in the state.

Dairy farming is by far the most significant contributor to Vermont's agricultural sector. Annual sales of milk, cheese, ice cream, and other dairy products from Vermont total about $1.2 billion. Vermont is also a leading producer of maple syrup and maple sugar.

Tourism is very important to Vermont's economy. Each year, more than 13 million people visit the Green Mountain State, and they spend some $1.4 billion in the process. Vermont is a magnet for skiers and snowboarders during the winter months. In summer, tourists come to experience the state's quaint towns and beautiful scenery. In fall, Vermont's forests are ablaze with color, and hordes of people visit to see the gorgeous foliage.

Vermont's legislature holds its sessions in the historic State House in Montpelier, which was built in the 1850s. The building also includes a ceremonial office for the state governor to use when signing legislation.

Burlington, on the eastern shore of Lake Champlain, is Vermont's largest city. This view shows the Burlington boat marina, with city buildings in the background.

Montpelier, on the Winooski River in central Vermont, has fewer residents than any other state capital in the United States.

The People

Americans increasingly are living in densely populated urban areas. In 2010, according to the U.S. Census Bureau, 8 in 10 Americans lived in such an area. Vermont is a notable exception to that trend. The Census Bureau found that 61.1 percent of Vermonters lived in a rural area in 2010. Only Maine had a higher proportion of rural residents (61.3 percent).

In all, about 626,000 people live in Vermont. That makes Vermont the country's second smallest state by population. As is the case with the other states of northern New England, Vermont's people are overwhelmingly white. According to the Census Bureau, non-Hispanic whites make up 94 percent of the Green Mountain State's population. The majority are of French/French Canadian, English, or Irish ancestry.

African Americans make up just 1.1 percent of Vermont's population. The proportion of Latinos (1.6 percent) and Asians (1.4 percent) is only slightly higher.

Major Cities

With a population of more than 42,000, **Burlington** is Vermont's largest city. Located on the eastern shore of Lake Champlain, it's the county seat of Chittenden County. It's also home to the University of Vermont, which has a total enrollment of about 12,000.

Bordering its namesake on the south and east, **South Burlington** is Vermont's second largest city. It has about 18,000 residents.

The county seat of north-central Vermont's Washington County, **Montpelier** has also served as the permanent state capital since 1808. Montpelier is the smallest state capital in the country. The 2010 census counted just 7,855 residents.

Further Reading

Bushnell, Mark. *It Happened in Vermont*. Guilford, CT: Globe Pequot, 2009.

Haugen, Brenda. *Ethan Allen: Green Mountain Rebel*. Mankato, MN: Compass Point Books, 2005.

Heinrichs, Ann. *Vermont*. New York: Scholastic, 2009.

Internet Resources

http://vermonthistory.org/explorer/this-day-in-history/vermont-timeline

This interactive timeline is maintained by the Vermont Historical Society.

http://www.vtstateparks.com/

The website of Vermont's Department of Forests, Parks, and Recreation offers photos, nature information, a monthly e-newsletter, and more.

https://www.sec.state.vt.us/kids/funfacts.html

Fun facts for kids, from the office of Vermont's Secretary of State.

 # Text-Dependent Questions

1. With which neighboring state does Vermont share Lake Chaplain?
2. What were the New Hampshire Grants?
3. What is unique about Montpelier?

 # Research Project

How do we know that Vermont is the nation's second least populous state, or that Burlington has more than 42,000 people, or that just over 1 percent of Vermonters are African American? Because the U.S. Census Bureau collects and analyzes all sorts of data about the country's people. Find out about your community using the Census Bureau's QuickFacts website, http://quickfacts.census.gov/qfd/index.html.

Index

Numbers in **bold italics** refer to captions.

Series Glossary of Key Terms

bicameral—having two legislative chambers (for example, a senate and a house of representatives).

cede—to yield or give up land, usually through a treaty or other formal agreement.

census—an official population count.

constitution—a written document that embodies the rules of a government.

delegation—a group of persons chosen to represent others.

elevation—height above sea level.

legislature—a lawmaking body.

precipitation—rain and snow.

term limit—a legal restriction on how many consecutive terms an office holder may serve.